314136

John Dewey's Challenge
to Education

John Dewey's Challenge to Education

Historical Perspectives on the Cultural Context

by

OSCAR HANDLIN

Foreword by
ARTHUR G. WIRTH
*Chairman, The John Dewey Society
Commission on Publications*

WITHDRAWN

GREENWOOD PRESS, PUBLISHERS
WESTPORT, CONNECTICUT

The Library of Congress cataloged this book as follows:

Handlin, Oscar, 1915–
    John Dewey's challenge to education; historical perspec-
tives on the cultural context. Foreword by Arthur G.
Wirth. Westport, Conn., Greenwood Press ₁1971, c1959₁

    59 p. 23 cm.

    Original ed. issued as no. 2 of The John Dewey Society lecture-
ship series.
    Includes bibliographical references.

    1. Dewey, John, 1859–1952.   I. Series: The John Dewey So-
ciety lectureship series.

LB875.D5H28   1971   370.1′092′4   71–138145
ISBN 0–8371–5602–5   MARC

Library of Congress   72 ₍4₎   ›

Originally published in 1959 by Harper & Brothers.

Reprinted with the permission of Harper & Row, Publishers

Reprinted in 1971 by Greenwood Press,
a division of Congressional Information Service, Inc.
88 Post Road West, Westport, Connecticut 06881

Library of Congress catalog card number 71-138145
ISBN 0-8371-5602-5

Printed in the United States of America

10 9 8 7 6 5 4 3

Foreword

BY ARTHUR G. WIRTH
Chairman, the John Dewey Society
Commission on Publications

This second volume in the John Dewey Society Lecture Series[1] coincides with John Dewey Centennial celebrations which will be held on campuses throughout the country during the academic year 1959–1960. In keeping with the central intention of the Society which is to foster continuing study of the relation of education and culture, and the sources of a theory of education, the present volume hews rigorously to the canons of careful scholarship in providing an insightful understanding of the American school and its cultural context at the beginning of Dewey's career. Professor Handlin's study is not concerned with eulogizing the man but succeeds in an unusual manner in casting useful light on a significant moment in our educational history. The fresh perspective that is created is particularly useful at the end of the present decade.

The debate on education in the period just behind us has been one of the most clamorous in the history of a people whose differences over matters of educational policy often have been stormy. While there has been much that has been exacerbating in the controversy, one result has been that the urgency of the problems of American education has been called forcibly to public attention.

[1] The first volume: Ordway Tead, *The Climate of Learning: A Constructive Attack on Complacency in Higher Education.* The John Dewey Society Lectureship—Number One (New York: Harper and Brothers, 1958).

· 5 ·

A fuller explanation of the factors responsible for the depths of personal passion involved and the sharp clash of opinions must remain a necessary and important subject for future investigations. It seems safe to hazard a guess or two, however, as to the factors responsible for the harsh quality that prevailed.

The 1950's saw a public school system, suffering from malnourishment and neglect, called on to meet demands unprecedented in scope and dimension. These demands derived in turn from the needs of an America being radically transformed by a myriad of social changes, most of which could be traced to the shock effects of an ever-accelerating scientific-technological revolution. Strange and weighty responsibilities were being required of a people vaulted to the front ranks of world leadership in a period fraught with grave and continuing crises at home and abroad. No institution escaped the consequences of pervasive change. The erosion of cherished values and the conflict of new and old were at work in all phases of our lives. The frustrating confrontation of the ideology and power of international communism was only the most obvious of the many challenges before us. While a serious threat in itself, a sometimes morbid concentration with it led to the obscuring of the true dimensions of other compelling problems.

Because of bewilderment over the magnitude and complexity of the issues, there was a tendency to seek oversimplified causes. There was, for example, the search for sinister forces or figures which, when exposed, might provide visible explanations for our ills. Such attempts at exorcism of evil spirits proved to be a poor substitute for serious, analytical thought.

On the educational scene it is common knowledge that John Dewey was frequently cast in the role of the *bête noire* responsible in some devious way for all the shortcomings of American schools. The chief victim of this sloganeering type of thinking was not John Dewey, whose reputation will outlive that of critics of this caliber, but American education itself, which was denied for awhile the responsible, probing kind of thinking it so sorely needed.

We may hope that we are through the worst of that period and that the time for a more mature assessment is at hand. A necessary part of such an appraisal must include a critical evaluation of the strengths and inadequacies of John Dewey's contributions to American educational thought as we seek out policies appropriate for the times upon us.

It is the conviction of this Society that Professor Handlin's present study makes a useful and constructive contribution to this end. It is noticeably free from strident defensiveness. The goal is to provide us with a measure of understanding about the social and educational context existing in the years preceding and following the turn of the century—and to elucidate the relation of this setting to Dewey's work.

Professor Handlin's training and professional career have provided him with admirable equipment for the task at hand. At present he is a member of the Department of History at Harvard University. Upon graduating from Brooklyn College in 1934 he pursued graduate studies at Harvard University where his attention was directed by distinguished mentors to the subjects of social history which have continued to occupy much of his attention. In 1941 he received the John H. Dunning Prize of the American Historical Association for his study, *Boston's Immigrants, 1790-1865; A Study of Acculturation,* and a Pulitzer Prize in 1952 for *The Uprooted,* a sensitive, insightful study of the social and personal problems of American immigrants.

His long list of publications, in which his wife Mary often collaborated, includes such works as *Adventure in Freedom, Danger in Discord, Race and Nationality in American Life, Al Smith and His America,* and *The America People in the Twentieth Century.* Scheduled for publication in 1959 is *The Newcomers: Negroes and Puerto Ricans in a Changing Metropolis.* This latter is one volume in the massive Harvard University Study known as the New York Metropolitan Region Study conducted by the Regional Plan Association.

Professor Handlin, as a long-time student of the causes and

consequences of institutional and cultural change, mines the kinds of material overlooked by less perceptive scholars. In the process, the current nostalgic view of the stern virtues of the school of the good old days is exposed as one of those wishful illusions far removed from the concrete reality of the times. We are led to see that the school at the end of the nineteenth century in actuality was floundering for lack of a sense of bearing. Its often effete, small-town characteristics, which it inherited from a fast-receding past, made its efforts remote and ineffective for the masses of children then crowding into the new urban schools. It made, in fact, for the "waste in education" on which Dewey elaborated in his little volume *The School and Society.* It was a school out of touch with the dominant, emerging social realities of a metropolitan, scientific, industrialized America. The democratic values themselves were in urgent need of re-examination if they were to have genuine relevancy for the new conditions of life. Until clarification in this area was advanced, the central purposes of the school would be obscured. It was to these critical questions that Dewey directed his attention.

If we continue to live with many of these questions in an acute form, we need not feel cheated that Dewey did not provide us with the finished answers. It was his major contribution that he progressively clarified the nature of the problems to be confronted. He engaged in exploring them in a refreshing, thought-provoking way, and reminded us constantly that the task of seeking out salutary relationships between patterns of education and the values of free men in a radically changing world is a continuing obligation.

Uncompromising candor and disciplined thinking are the indispensable requirements. The heritage of John Dewey is betrayed primarily when we turn aside from the arduous task of inquiring into the genuine problems posed by new realities and resort to cliché-ridden sloganeering. Both followers and critics of Dewey would do themselves profit by frequently reminding themselves of this fact.

A happy consequence of Professor Handlin's study is its reminder that Dewey followed his own advice. He committed himself to the rejection of hackneyed, stereotyped views of the world in which he lived. He sought to ferret out the actual factors that were transforming social life and to raise questions regarding the consequences, on the assumption that more authentic life-meanings could be secured only as these painful operations uncompromisingly were pursued. This task remains for us in our time.

The present Chairman of the Commission on Publications took over his duties after Professor Handlin had been commissioned to prepare this lecture. He wishes to acknowledge his special debts to Professor William O. Stanley, who secured the services of the author of this volume, and to Professor William Van Til, who as Acting President of the Society in the absence of Professor H. Gordon Hullfish, on leave in Japan, was an indispensable source of guidance and support. Finally, he wishes to express his gratitude to Professor Archibald Anderson, long-time editor of *Educational Theory,* and the preceding Chairman of the John Dewey Society Commission on Publication. It was under his leadership that the present plan of publications of the Society took shape.[2] The John Dewey Society is now engaged in establishing two new publications series.

One of these is the *John Dewey Society Studies in Educational Theory.* The central purpose of this series will be to provide vigorous and creative study of the theoretical foundations of education as demanded by the present situation. One or two authors will be commissioned to pursue such inquiries.

The other is the John Dewey Lectureship Series of which the present volume is the second. This is to consist of the printed version of an annual lecture to be delivered by some outstanding individual, either in or outside the field of education, whose ideas can be useful in stimulating thought about the theoretical and practical problems of education. In order

[2] For an elaboration of the work of the John Dewey Society and its program of publications, see Archibald Anderson, "Fostering Study in the Theory of Education: The Development of New Approaches to Basic Educational Problems," *Educational Theory,* January 1959, pp. 16 ff.

to provide a proper forum for what is intended to be a significent statement on education, a cooperative arrangement with the National Society of Teachers of Education has been arranged so that this organization makes available each year one of the general sessions of its annual convention for the presentation of the John Dewey Society Lecture.

Preface

Although the address contained in this volume was prepared for the 1959 meeting of the John Dewey Society, the
material that is in it was collected over a long period. My
attention was first called to these problems when I spoke
to the 1956 meeting of the Southern Historical Association
on "The Role of Science in the 1890's." I touched on other
phases of the subject in a paper on "The Immigrant and
American Education" delivered to the American Historical
Association in 1957. Some aspects of the analysis of culture
were developed in a Blazer Lecture at the University of
Kentucky in 1958. The final work on the paper was done in
connection with studies that arose out of the work of the
Center for the Study of the History of Liberty in America at
Harvard University.

I am grateful to the officers of the John Dewey Society
for presenting me with the occasion for expressing my
thoughts on this aspect of American education as well as
to the sponsors of the other meetings and to the discussants
who participated in them for many stimulating comments.

In the course of these years, I have been helped also by
the criticisms of Professor Paul H. Buck and Professor Bernard

Bailyn of Harvard University, of Professor John Higham of Rutgers University, and of Professor Merle Borrowman of the University of Wisconsin.

As has so often been the case in the past, Mary Flug Handlin shared fully in the research and writing of this study. Dorothy Summers prepared the manuscript with efficiency and dispatch.

Oscar Handlin

Harvard University
May 11, 1959

John Dewey's Challenge
to Education

THE IMPORTANCE OF THE CONTEXT

The simplicity of historical chronology is often deceptive. It is tempting but dangerous to hang the interpretation of a long-term development upon a succession of striking events. We know, for example, that John Dewey opened his experimental school at the University of Chicago in 1896. In 1904 he went to Columbia University. His *Democracy and Education* was published in 1916; and three years later the Progressive Education Association was established. The direct line from date to date lends plausibility to the assertion that the progressive movement in education began in 1896 and grew steadily thereafter. Thence it is but a short step to holding Dewey responsible for everything that has happened to American education since 1896.

This trap has claimed some of Dewey's defenders and many of his critics. Recent comments all too often leave the impression that the schools since the 1890's have been entirely dominated by "progressive" ideas or by "Deweyism." Actually, it has been shown that while Dewey and others were thinking along lines that might be called progressive in the 1890's, their theories were not widely spread until after the first world war; and their genuine importance came much later still. It is fallacious to ascribe either the evils or the virtues of American education before 1917 to progressive education or to John Dewey.[1]

This clarification is not merely a matter of setting the historical record straight. It is also essential in comprehending the significance of Dewey's ideas. The movement in which he played a part has often been described as a revolt. But to understand its character it is necessary to begin by recognizing the established patterns against which the revolt was directed. Yet the central features of the *ancien régime* in American education are but vaguely remembered; otherwise we would not now hear so much talk of the return to a "good old system" that was neither good nor old—nor indeed, much of a system. This paper will outline the social and cultural context of American education in the period between 1870 and 1910, in order to make clear the shortcomings against which Dewey and his collaborators directed their criticism. Only in the light of that context does the significance of progressive education become meaningful.

The forty years after 1870 were a period of critical change, both in the nation and in its schools. Unfortunately, although for reasons which are themselves important, there was a vast discrepancy between what happened to the schools and what happened to the nation. The development of education, shaped by the ideals of an earlier America, opened a widening gap between the school and the society evolving around it and created burdensome problems for both. It was against the unwillingness to face those problems, many of which plague us still, that Dewey revolted. We shall not understand either his revolt or the problems themselves without understanding first the context within which both developed.

❦

CHANGES IN SCHOOLS AND NATION

These four decades witnessed a radical transformation in American education. The number of students rose steadily, driven upward by the growth of population through natural increment and through immigration. The concentration of an ever larger percentage of the population in urban places and the extension of the duration of schooling also contributed to the increase. The result was a marked, if chaotic, attempt to clarify the functions of the schools at every level. Rapid changes in the curriculum and continuous, agitated questioning about the character of education reflected a pervasive uncertainty concerning the proper purpose and even the proper form of these institutions. "A thorough, orderly, and scientific organization of education is at length needed," complained W. W. Folwell in 1875.[2] By the end of the century such an orderly structure was defined, in a pattern still recognizable today. The schools were public, secular, compulsory, and free; and they fell into the three-fold division of elementary, secondary, and higher.[3]

In the same forty years, however, the United States also changed. Its empty continental spaces rapidly filled up as railroads bound the nation together. Its population more than doubled, with an ever larger percentage of its residents concentrated in great metropolitan centers rather than spread across the rural countryside. Its wealth more often was drawn

· 17 ·

from factories, manned by a depressed labor force, than from the farms of independent husbandmen. Its economic, cultural, and political interests stretched far beyond the limits of the two oceans. The life of the men who were shortly to confront a world war was thus radically different from that of their forebears who had emerged from the Civil War.

The human beings who suffered the shock of these cataclysmic changes could not immediately adjust their habits of thought and action to the new circumstances. To many contemporaries the nation seemed to be "whirling down the descending grade to destruction." The signs of its peril were unwieldy populations crowded into great cities and factories, the loss of the sense of individual responsibility in the face of the complex issues of modern life, materialism and excessive ambition, and the immense social gulf between "the apes of fashion and the reckless horde." The result was that liberty was mistaken for license, the anarchist and capitalist alike defied the government, and mobs hissed the American flag.[4]

At the heart of these complaints was a sense of communal disintegration. The shock of the Civil War produced social effects felt for decades thereafter. Industrialization, the development of massive metropolitan centers, the creation of gigantic fortunes in the hands of new men, the peculiar conditions of life on the prairie farms, the undermining of family relations over a whole continent, and the attenuation of supernatural beliefs in religion—all these were factors in the cataclysmic collapse of communal institutions. And that collapse accounted for the sense of drift and lack of guidance or standards so characteristic of these years.[5]

Under these circumstances, the common assumption was

that it was the duty of the school to intervene, to supply the guides to action that the individual could no longer acquire through the slow accretion of experiences, to impart the instruction that the family and the church had offered in more stable societies and that now were simply lacking.[6]

President Charles W. Eliot of Harvard University summarized the need most cogently: "In spite of every effort to enlighten the whole body of the people, all sorts of quacks and impostors thrive. . . . The astrologer in the Middle Ages was a rare personage . . . but now he advertises in the public newspapers and flourishes as never before. Men and women of all classes . . . seek advice . . . from clairvoyants, seers, Christian Scientists, mind-cure practitioners . . . and fortune tellers. The ship of state barely escapes from one cyclone of popular folly, like the fiat-money delusion or the granger legislation of the seventies, when another blast of ill-informed opinion comes down on it, like the actual legislation which compels the buying and storing of silver by Government."[7] It was the same "in this matter of aesthetics." Popular tastes were hopeless; a fresh start with the children was essential.[8]

The very statement of the problem hinted at the answer. Experience could not be counted on to endow a man with the cultural equipment for life's decisions. The school would have to do so.

❧

THE SCHOOL AS PREPARATION FOR LIFE

The task of the schools was commonly described as that of preparing its students for life, an admirable general proposition with which few could disagree. Yet the meaning of the phrase became alarmingly elusive when efforts were made to reduce it to concrete terms. It could variously be applied to readiness for further education, to the acquisition of a trade, to training for citizenship, and to equipment with a general culture. The ambiguity is significant and deserves extended examination.

The analysis which follows could apply to every aspect of American education in this period. But it will focus primarily upon the high school, to which, in these years, all other levels of teaching accommodated themselves.

As the registration figures of the high schools soared after 1870, the academies of an earlier period declined precipitously in number and in influence. Few survived unless they were able to transform themselves into select college preparatory schools, specializing in the training of the sons of elite men of wealth.[9] As a result the colleges were deprived of students prepared to carry on the existing courses of study; and they ultimately adjusted their instruction to the level of preparation provided by the high school. A system of accrediting standardized a uniform pattern of preparation. No longer did a boy enter by examination whenever he was ready; he now did so when he left high school.[10] In the same way the high school shaped the character of the elementary instruction by regularizing the eight-year primary course that supplied it with students.[11]

Yet the high school was not simply an institution that completed the studies of the elementary school, nor yet simply one that initiated the studies of college. It did both, and more besides. The commonly expressed views as to its complex functions reveal some of the American expectations of education at the close of the nineteenth century.[12]

The high school tried to prepare some of its students for college. Yet the preponderant number of graduates did not go on, and the percentage who did so remained relatively unchanged in this period. Such considerations led the National Education Association's Committee of Ten on Secondary School Studies to conclude that the program of these institutions ought to be designed "for those children whose education is not to be pursued beyond the secondary school. The preparation of a few pupils for college or scientific school should . . . be the incidental, and not the principal object."[13] That judgment reflected the existing situation; high school instruction was not primarily shaped to fit some students for college.

In the beginning, indeed, this had been regarded as a terminal institution to equip young men with trades; and its objective continued to be, in part at least, vocational training. Rapid economic change stimulated a demand for the "opportunity of learning how to do more and better work"; and courses in the manual and mercantile arts had demonstrable utility.[14] Low wages, it was argued, were not due to the capitalist or to society but to faulty education. Particularly since the old system of apprenticeship was declining, it was "the duty of the state, as a business manager," to establish secondary technical schools in order to assure the nation's industrial supremacy. A careful development of "country schools preparatory to agriculture" and city schools preparatory "to the mechanic and manufacturing arts" would assure the efficient application of science to the productive system.[15]

However, there was a seemingly irresistible trend toward

the perversion of vocational into general courses. No sooner was a trade inserted into the curriculum than its sponsors began to urge it as a study upon all children. It was a truism that every boy ought to be taught to work—even, some said, before he was taught to read. Such training bridged over social cleavages, inculcated a love of labor, prevented idleness, and might be useful in later life. About the story of a clerk who took the place of a striking blacksmith and saved the day for the construction company, the editor moralized, "By his manual training that lad had become an American of the old school."[16]

Some educational theorists had always given high value to the cultural implications of manual training. But the insistence that such courses were general deprived them of their vocational character, in a process similar to that which was also turning the land-grant colleges away from their original purpose.[17] The labor unions were therefore frequently hostile; and artisans and craftsmen continued to learn their trades at the bench rather than in the classroom. Significantly, the popular conception of success rarely ascribed a man's rise in the world to the quality of his education.[18]

Vocational education was pushed toward the general because it was oriented toward the past rather than toward the present. There were frequent verbal acknowledgments that the struggle for existence was becoming fiercer in consequence of the denser population and the disappearance of the empty lands of the frontier and that therefore, "Our artisans and mechanics must be trained to compete with those from the technical and industrial schools of European countries."[19] But in practice the schools did not conceive it their function to prepare students for the jobs the economy actually offered. They hoped rather to preserve the archaic handicraft skills of a productive system that was already disappearing. This function then was detached from the actualities of life outside the school.

❧

EDUCATING CITIZENS

Preparation for life had a wider meaning also. The schools, as "an element of national strength," had an obligation to train good citizens. The only justification for taking "the people's money for public instruction," it was often said in these years, was that the common school was "the corner-stone of our national order of Republican society."[20]

There had been a time, of course, when education had not been deemed essential to good citizenship. Back in 1798, William Manning had argued that learning was actually a threat to democracy. Every yeoman knew his own interests, and schooling was not likely to further his capacity to act intelligently in politics. As late as 1871 Governor Brown of Missouri still denied there was a connection between education and citizenship and pointed out, "Your prime rascals are educated rascals."[21]

Well before the Civil War, this assurance had begun to fade. Instead, the spread of public education was justified by the contention that the good citizen needed some minimal schooling to understand his own and his country's interests. Only thus could he act intelligently on the manifold issues of public policy decided by his vote.[22] In the closing decades

· 23 ·

of the century the change went much farther. It was no longer enough to give each citizen the ability to read, and to count on him then "to cast the ballot intelligently and wisely." The function of the schools was to indoctrinate their students with a positive pattern of beliefs, "political and moral axioms and principles" that would guide their acts as citizens. There were even proposals that only those so educated should be allowed to vote.[23]

This conception received formal expression at the hands of the Herbartians. If one could teach morals through literature and history, then it followed that those subjects should so be taught as to imbue the young with the moral values upon which the society agreed. It was a short step from that point to J. B. McMaster's conclusion that history was to teach Americans the lofty ideals by which the United States had always been animated. Furthermore, almost every subject could be related to the same end. Even physical education was justified on the ground that it developed a sense of discipline and respect for law; and there were discussions as to which of the sports was most "fully in accord with the Zeitgeist."[24] Thus, education for citizenship became identified with patriotism. It was the task of the schools, through moral and intellectual training, to impart to the child that love of country which was the only reliable basis of correct political action.[25]

The conflation of these values and emotions was evident in the Columbian Public Schools Celebration of 1892. Initiated by the magazine *Youth's Companion*, the idea for a mammoth commemoration of the four-hundredth anniversary of the discovery of America was taken up by the National Convention of Superintendents of Education and sanctioned by an act of Congress. During the course of the celebration there was a significant association of Columbus, the flag, and the public schools. The public schools, symbolized by the "little red schoolhouse" in the parades, were "the noblest expression of the principle of enlightenment which Columbus grasped by faith, . . . the master force which, under God, has been informing each of our generations with the peculiar truths of Americanism." The mere flying of the flag "over the schoolhouses, also, impressed powerfully upon the youth that we are a nation," and developed "brave manly boys and womanly girls."[26]

The flag had itself by now become an object of ritual veneration. Careful consideration was given to ceremonies that would stimulate the respect of the young. The fervent quality of this iconoduly may be gauged from the horrified comments of an editor who observed a group of New England boys throwing snowballs at some girls in sight of the flag. "The American flag means fair play, equal chance, protection of the weak, . . . honor to women." In hoisting the flag, "the pupils of the school make a profession of the American religion, a leading principle of which is respect and consideration" for women.[27]

Yet even that editor was, on occasion, forced to acknowledge that raising the flag was not enough. "Genuine love of country" called not only for the "recitation of deeds of heroism and past public service," through literature and history. It called also for "a special tie to the soil—a feeling which allies itself to the trees, the flowers, the birds, the prairies . . . the hills, the wild creatures of the woods and fields, and everything that is distinctively American."[28]

The concealed premise of this statement—that it was possible to define a homogeneous pattern of American emotions and attitudes—ran counter to all the changes that made American life more heterogeneous through these decades. Sectional, ethnic and urban-rural divisions were becoming more rather than less pronounced. Yet the schools continued to cling to uniformity as an ideal toward which their students were to be trained.

That insistence was most clearly revealed in attitudes toward the immigrants. There were, of course, exceptional teachers who appreciated the distinctive qualities of their foreign-born pupils and who rose to the challenge of working with them.[29] But the predominant view was that under the impact of a "flood of imported barbarism" the "whole upper strata of society" were "becoming debauched." Fear of the consequences led sober, law-abiding men to go so far as to justify the lynching of Italians in New Orleans.[30]

Although their children were but a small proportion of the school population, the newcomers were often described as a "distinct national menace." No one could live exposed to them without infection. They were making "a sorry mess" of the nation's language, for instance. "Their speech," to which they stubbornly clung, was "but a mangled product" of "fragments from many tongues." To permit them thus to corrupt English was disloyal and unpatriotic.[31]

The foreigners not only perverted American tastes; they also brought with them an "antagonism to fixed institutions and ideas," and they actually led the native-born into idleness and crime. "All the trade unions of the country are controlled by foreigners," *The Century* explained. "While they refuse admission to the trained American boy, they admit all foreign applicants with little or no regard to their training or skill." Hence the susceptibility of American young men to idleness, crime, and error.[32]

Thus in discussions of the function of the schools, civic education was as little related to the needs of the present as vocational training. In reference to both, the assumption prevailed that it was desirable to cut the school apart from the main currents of the life about it. That assumption did not arise merely out of respect for an archaic past. It was rather the product of a newly developed view of culture and of its place in the curriculum.

❦

CULTURE AND THE CURRICULUM

It was all very well to assert that the truly good citizen was "a man of large sympathies," educated to have a wide familiarity in the sciences and arts.[33] Such general statements met with universal assent, for culture was conceded to be a universal good. Almost as a matter of course the schools, and particularly the high schools, accepted the task of educating young people in that sense. The importance of that function will become clear from a concrete examination of precisely what culture the schools transmitted to students through the evolving curriculum of these years.

The course of study was at no time the logically structured entity it has sometimes appeared to be in retrospect.[34] The actual curriculum of the high school, for instance, was a conglomeration of traditional and new materials inserted or retained in the adjustment to a variety of pressures. In discerning the relationship of education to culture, however, these pressures are less significant than the means by which they were rationalized. There was an intense rivalry among all teachers to further their own subjects. But there was a striking uniformity to the justifications they gave for them. All argued that their subjects were part of the American's general equipment in dealing with his life's problems. No subject was to be taught merely, or primarily, because of the inherent importance of its content, but rather because of its contribution to an arsenal of weapons with which to deal with those problems. That was why the Committee of Ten recommended that "the best course of study" even for "the future common laborer" was a "portion of the longer course of study designed to educate the professional man."[35]

That was also why President Eliot had criticized the older curricula. "No amount of such studies will protect one from believing in astrology, or theosophy, or free silver, or strikes or boycotts, or in the persecution of Jews or of Mormons or in the violent exclusion of non-union men from employment." He himself thought, and many agreed with him, that only the sciences which gave men "practice in classification and induction" could impart the methods of right reasoning.[36]

Science was not, however, to be narrowly limited to the physical or natural sciences. "All sciences," it was agreed, "involve the same methods and employ the same faculties."[37] Mathematics was obviously useful for its training in logic.[38] History too had become a science with a laboratory method of its own; a well-known textbook aimed to train the pupil to think for himself "by giving him as material for his work,

Historical Sources."[39] And claims of equal validity were made for "the most difficult science of government and lawmaking" and for economics and social science.[40] As a matter of fact the identical case was made for domestic science and a multitude of other subjects.

Often, however, simple instruction in the correct procedures seemed inadequate. It was not enough to teach children who lived in slums that "a healthful, beautiful location, good construction, perfect drainage, perfect plumbing, and perfect sanitary conditions generally, are indispensable to the house beautiful"; or to illustrate the proper mode of dining with quotations from Homer, Plutarch, and Boswell.[41] It was essential, in addition, that the students' tastes be bent toward desirable, and therefore previously defined, goals.

Thus the function of the school was also to soften and ennoble its charges. "Beware of the boy who was never in love with his schoolmistress; he will become a man who will bear vigorous watching, even in the pulpit."[42] That end could be attained through the development of an appreciation of the higher aspects of culture. Domestic science, for instance, led to an awareness of the artistic elements in decoration and to an understanding of the beauties of English, French, German, and Italian furniture. Students were thus to be exposed to the noble, gentle styles of life so different from their own.[43]

The development of high school education in music was particularly enlightening from this point of view. The underlying emphasis at the start, and for a long time thereafter, was upon singing for an uplifting purpose. "We need more songs of home, of country, of simple praise to God and love to man."

Singing was important because of its subject matter. It dealt with "such subjects as Love of Country, Home-loving, the Golden Rule, etc." These, the teachers knew, "will surely develop like sentiments in the children who sing them." Since music regulated the emotions, "the habitual use of vocal music by a family" was "an almost unfailing sign of good morals and refined tastes."[44]

Furthermore, music also had value "as a disciplinary study" with power "to develop the mind and will of the child." It taught patriotism, morality, temperance, and obedience to the law. Singing was even "to some degree a safeguard against those diseases which affect the breathing organs." The need for proper attention to music was particularly great in the United States. "The social results of a developed rhythmical sense in considerable masses of people . . . are far-reaching. It cultivates a feeling for order and regularity. . . . It gives . . . a measure of values. . . . With our heterogeneous population, our widespread opposition of social classes, and the dreadful monotony of living among the lower classes . . . it surely is worth our while to cultivate in all classes and in every kind of social group the feeling for order and symmetry." A "refined sense of harmony" was also essential. "The street noises that assault our ears and exhaust our nerves; the hideous architecture of our great cities, and the deadly architectural monotony of our factory towns; the excesses of public advertising; and our widespread disregard for the natural beauties of land, river and sea,—what are these but the inevitable outspeakings of a people to whom life has not yet became harmonious?"[45]

In the logical progression of this argument, music had become not that which people enjoyed, but that which was good for them. A little story made this unmistakably clear. The young girl, sent by the town's subscriptions to study at the Conservatory in Boston, returns to Auroraville. Asked to play "Home, Sweet Home" or "Rocked in the Cradle of the Deep," she refuses: "You see, I have really learned what is good music." The townspeople are antagonized when she plays instead Moszkowski's Sonata, an "unmelodious, incomprehensible clatter." They withdraw their support. But she persists; and in time they acknowledge that they were wrong and she was right. "The people of no town were ever prouder of a native who had won distinction than the Auroraville people now are of that brilliant performer on the piano, Miss Hettie Ketchum."[46]

The result, in the schools, was a steady shift in emphasis to courses that would identify good music and bring "added culture and refinement" into children's nature.[47] It followed also that musicians had to avoid the opprobrium "of being deficient in general culture."[48]

So too, the teaching of art was desirable because it encouraged accuracy of observation and contributed to success in later life. But the objects had to be carefully chosen; in a defective painting, the effect was "exactly like that of powder and rouge on a woman's face."[49] "The purification and elevation" of "a vitiated and crude public taste" was "manifestly to be achieved by the systematic education of the youth" in the appreciation of great art, "however difficult that might be."[50]

But above all else, a knowledge of great literature was important. "Literature," said Professor Woodrow Wilson, "will keep us pure and keep us strong."[51] "Literature is a power," said the financier to the aspiring young hero in a novel.[52] It could rescue the language from the deterioration with which it was threatened. Journalistic style, "short, direct talk," and passages "characterized by terse sentences" were corrupting the written language as books became sensational and magazines were marred with pictures and headlines. The spoken language was even worse. The old-time preaching and oratory were out of fashion and slang intruded into conversation. Yet "vocal form," Henry James pointed out, was "the touchstone of manners" and the symbol of civilization. Under these circumstances the teaching of good literature, of good speech, even of how to read a good newspaper were inescapable duties of the school.[53]

There was a common assumption concealed in all these obligations loaded upon the school. When the teacher asserted that cleanliness, order, and honesty were basic to art, or when she was instructed, "In discussing beautiful objects as distinguished from those which are simply gaudy, it will be better to borrow objects from the stores, as we do not wish to criticize objects which the children bring from their own homes," it was an affirmation that the culture communicated through the school was unrelated to the life of its students. The teacher might hope that the good influences he generated would spread to the homes and elevate the parents. But figuratively and actually, he envisioned the school as cut off from, and battling against, the dominant currents of the civilization within which it existed.[54]

CULTURE AND SOCIETY

The culture communicated by the schools had thus become entirely detached from experience. The disjunction was not the product of forces peculiar to education. It sprang rather from the rapid changes of the period in the whole social context of the nation.

The term culture, as commonly used in the schools and outside them, comprehended the possession of knowledge through science as a guide to right action in every sphere of personal and social life. But it also included the possession of certain symbols of gentility and quality, primarily in the arts. Medicine or economics or natural science supplied the right answers to questions of health or business or the character of the natural universe; and music or painting or literature supplied the right modes of emotional expression.

To discriminate right from wrong in science or art, however, was by no means easy. Social science and Christian Science, phrenology and zoology and astrology all justified their claims with their own credentials. Why should one believe in a neolithic age but not in a lost continent of Atlantis? A scientific magazine discussed the birds of the grasslands and a new star in the Milky Way, the conservation of the mackerel supply and the cabalistic shapes numbers naturally assumed. All were science.[55] And, alas, the confusion of claims in the arts was more confounded still. Some standard of judgment was desperately required.

The urgency was most acute among men and women of wealth, whether inherited or newly acquired. Such people were most sensitive to the need for dependable criteria of thought and action. They lived always under the pressure of insecurity about their possessions and of uncertainty about how to play their own roles. Their frenetic eagerness to develop a "Society" was an effort to bring into being the norms that would determine who belonged and who did not and that would establish the appropriate modes of thought and behavior. Reluctant to base status solely upon riches, which were easily gained and lost, those who aspired to leadership wished to make the possession of culture one of the major tests for admission to, or exclusion from, Society.[56] "Changes in manners and customs," Edith Wharton had said, "originate with the wealthy or aristocratic minority, and are thence transmitted to the other classes." It was thus the responsibility of Society to provide cultural guidance to the nation.[57]

The years after 1870 saw the development and elaboration of an apparatus for defining the official culture of this Society. It included institutions like museums, symphony orchestras, opera companies, and learned societies; and an array of journals and publications that passed judgment on taste and ideas. This apparatus was in the hands of a few key figures, the critics and influential scholars who were the ultimate arbiters. The critic in this role was the source of discipline, the man who "screws down the brakes," rather than "the sentimentalist irresponsibly swept into folly by the fury of the crowd, or the demagogue whooping its shibboleth."[58] At the core of this apparatus was the university, in which science and art were joined. In its development, Society shared the control and supplied the funds; and in return it sought and generally, although not always, secured a certified set of standards it could accept. The union of the college and the university in a manner unique to the United States significantly reflected the function they were to serve. The university defined taste and knowledge while the college imparted them to the children of the elite, who were thereby set off as a group.[59]

The struggle to effect such a definition and to certify what was officially correct in this sense was fought in every field of American culture. It may most clearly be perceived in the fate of medical practice. By the end of the nineteenth century the dozens of medical sects that had formerly had respectable followings had been extinguished by state action and but "one mode of healing" had been given "exclusive control." That mode was one certified by approved medical schools and societies—that is, by those linked to the universities, by those whose practitioners had heeded the advice given to the Philadelphia medical students, that "Of all men, the medical practitioner should be, above all things, a perfect gentleman," and should "move only in the best, unquestioned society."[60] These institutions developed the practitioners influential in Society; and that influence brought them the victory of official and exclusive recognition.[61]

What happened in medicine happened also in the other professions. All came to recruit their practitioners from among the graduates of schools linked to the universities. Most of them achieved some degree of social and legal recognition through a formal process of certification; and in most of those callings the old pattern of relatively free access disappeared.[62]

More important, an analogous process, although without

legal sanctions, operated in all phases of American culture. No degree or certificate or qualifying examination, but a validating process no less formal and stringent marked out the music or painting or book that received an approved place in the culture.

It was more difficult to secure the acceptance of these standards by the population at large. The problem and its resolution were illustrated in a boys' story. Snobbish Schuyler Rivington of New York is appallingly unlovely in his contacts with the residents of a small western town. But he is redeemed in the eyes of the likable old lady who comes to the city to be cured of a brain illness. New York was "not all fashion and frivolity"; it was, after all, justified by "the science and knowledge stored in the great city."[63] Science, like the culture Hettie brought back from the conservatory in Boston, was perhaps hard to take. But it was good for you.

❦

THE SCHOOLS AND THE DIFFUSION OF CULTURE

And here we return to the schools and particularly to the high school. Their function was to diffuse the values of the officially defined culture. They did so not only by preparing some pupils for college but, more important, by securing the universal acceptance of the defined culture through their courses in science, history, politics, economics, art, music, and literature.

That acquiescense was secured because the school was also a significant channel of upward social mobility; American boys and girls were "all climbers upon a ladder."[64] Cautious protests that the school ought "not to push the pupil beyond his environment" had no effect.[65] Its very stucture and organization encouraged mobility. For students, the reward for accepting its values, that is for doing well, was access to the colleges, to the professions, and even to the opportunities business afforded. The reality of these rewards was an incentive of enormous attractiveness toward acceptance of the established cultural norms. The school thus permitted the wide diffusion of the officially defined culture with relatively little strain or tension.[66]

The more serious damage was to culture itself. Detached from their lives, it did not meet the needs of many Americans. While accepting the privileged status of that which was defined as culture, they turned for their own satisfaction and enjoyment to forms which developed outside the range of established controls, and to that extent, were popular. Only a "few people of refinement and culture" appreciated the best drama for "art's sake" and for its function "in educating the noblest faculties of the mind," a critic observed sadly. The masses went to the theater for entertainment, to gratify "exotic tendencies" and "to ease the stress of sensuous toil" when weary of "the hard, hopeless grind of business and household cares." Such people were not heedful of the critics. The theater they patronized developed spontaneously and independently.[67]

In the same way the popular medicine of unorthodox healers and patent medicines served more people than that of the M.D.; the popular sciences of the Sunday supplements convinced more readers than the official science of the learned journals; men sang and danced to popular music, however much they were taught to appreciate the official music of the schools. The dime novels and the magazines made popular a literature and art of which the critics took no cognizance at all. A perceptive observer, criticizing the methods of "Art Study" in 1906, pointed out, "The children are living with the houses and the furniture and the wallpaper—God help them!—and the Buster Browns and Nervy Nats of to-day, and the ever present influence of these will not be overcome by ignoring them and summoning Giotto and Velasquez for ten minutes from the past."[68]

This was evidence of a disjunction between popular and official culture. That separateness was new to American life. In its development American education had had an important part, although one but slightly perceived and but little understood by those who participated in it.

Conversely the gap between popular and official culture also affected education. Hostile critics complained of the tendency toward making "a sort of college" of the free public school by offering instruction in science, literature, music, and art and by tolerating fraternities and organized athletics.[69] The urban high school, in their view, offered "a four years' course in an institution modelled on the plan of the university-fitting school of a generation ago;—four years of cramming in Latin and mathematics, with a little dabbling in science and a mild flirtation with English literature."[70] Such cultural fripperies had no place in free education. "We have no right to appropriate a dollar of the people's money" to make "scholars, in the university sense." From this point of view, the "rage for intellectual culture" was "the Moloch in the American

· 38 ·

school-room," sought only by parents infuriated with ambition for their children.[71]

❦

DEWEY AND THE PROBLEMS OF EDUCATION

It was the achievement of John Dewey to have couched his criticism of the divorce between experience and education in more meaningful terms. His practical contact with the problems of the schools of the 1880's and 1890's stimulated his philosophical inquiries into the nature of knowledge; and his understanding of the learning process supplied a theoretical basis to his views on proper pedagogy. The development of his ideas was thus meaningfully related to the context of the times in which he lived.

When Dewey came as instructor to the University of Michigan in 1884, he brought with him intellectual attitudes shaped by two forces. His early upbringing in Vermont had been permissive to the point of chaos; the most valuable lessons he had learned had been outside the classroom and independently carried forth. His own training had thus been almost casual and had certainly been free of the rigidity to be imposed on American schools after 1870. Recollections of his experience as a student no doubt influenced his later critical view of what education was becoming in the last quarter of the nineteenth century.

His philosophical background also raised questions with regard to current assumptions. From his graduate work under George S. Morris at Johns Hopkins he carried away a commitment to Hegelian idealism, which nurtured his hostility to dualisms of every sort and left him dubious as to the validity of all such dichotomies as those between education or culture and society or life.[72]

But at Michigan, Dewey's formal philosophical views and his personal memories were challenged by the necessities of instruction and by his immersion in the life of a community. To make his ideas comprehensible to the young men and women in his classrooms was but a fraction of his task. In addition, he had to be aware of the relationship of his work to the world about him; and as a member of the faculty of a state university, he also had to concern himself with the problems of the public school system related to it. President Angell always regarded it as one of the chief duties of the university "to keep in close touch with the state system of public education." That preoccupation was reflected in Dewey's proposal to publish a general "Thought News"; and it emerged also in his earliest books, the core of which was analysis of the ways of knowing. The title of the volume in which he collaborated in 1889 was significant: *Applied Psychology: An Introduction to the Principles and Practices of Education.*[73]

His marriage in 1886 and the move to Chicago in 1894 added to the weight of the practical considerations in the development of his thought. The intellectual associations at the exciting new university were undoubtedly stimulating; but the exposure to the immediate problems of teaching in a great and expanding metropolis were fully as much so. Experiments in new education were already in progress in Chicago; and the Deweys at the Experimental School undoubtedly profited from them. But it is, in any case, clear that the main outlines of their work were set up on a pragmatic rather than a theoretical basis. That is, Dewey began to treat the problems of education not from an abstract, previously defined position of what ought ideally to be, but rather from a concrete estimate of deficiencies that actually existed.[74]

The systematic exploration of these problems did not follow until later. The first extensive exposition of Dewey's position came in the lectures collected as *The School and Society* (1899), a work which was still largely critical and negative. A fuller analysis appeared seventeen years later in *Democracy and Education*. But the general propositions enunciated in that work rested upon a very careful case by case study of particular experiments in the new education. Dewey's general conclusions were thus the products of more than twenty years of experience. His ideas were not formulated in the abstract but through the encounter with the conditions of learning in the United States in the closing decades of the nineteenth century.

The necessity for grappling with a development that had divorced the school and its culture from society and its life was an irritant that compelled Dewey to define his ideas on education. Those ideas were integrally related to his comprehensive conceptions of the character of knowledge, the mind, human nature, the experimental process, and the values of democracy. As he clarified his thoughts on education he also refined his views on these more general philosophical issues.[75]

But his conceptions also had a pragmatic attractiveness

that converted many Americans who did not accept or were unfamiliar with the wider implications of his philosophy. His ideas were persuasive because they revealed the evident weaknesses of the schools as they were.

❧

WHAT WAS WRONG WITH AMERICAN EDUCATION

The realm of the classroom in the 1890's was totally set off from the experience of the child who inhabited it. The teachers' lessons encrusted by habit, the seats arranged in formal rows, and the rigid etiquette of behavior all emphasized the difference between school and life. Hence learning consisted of the tedious memorization of data without a meaning immediately clear to the pupil.

Dewey, whose own education as a boy was free of all such rigidity, objected strenuously that these conditions stifled the learning process, for they prevented the student from relating his formal studies to his own development as a whole person.

The educator therefore had to narrow the distance between the classroom and the world outside it. Society was changing rapidly under the impact of urbanization and industrialization, and not always for the better. But the teacher ought not therefore pretend that his pupils still walked along the lanes of an eighteenth-century village back to a rustic farmhouse. He had to take account of the city streets and of the American home as it actually was.[76]

The educator could end the school's isolation by pulling it into a closer relationship with the family and the com-

munity. Awareness of the homes, the neighborhood environment, and the business and professional life about it would
enable the school to function more effectively and also to
widen its influence. By recognizing the unity of the child's
experience, it could communicate more directly with him
and at the same time break down the pernicious "division into
cultured people and workers." It would then cease to be
alien and hostile in the eyes of its students and become instead a natural part of their habitat within which they sought
satisfaction of their own needs.[77]

In such schools, the "subject matter in history and science
and art" could be so presented that it would have "a positive
value and a real significance in the child's own life." What
was taught would justify itself because it answered questions
the student himself asked. He would not be forced to study
the map to learn what the world was like; but exploring the
world about him, would come to wonder how it looked on
the map. History and literature would cease to be the elegant
furnishings of an abstract culture; the pupil would be drawn to
them out of his own desire to know himself and his origins.
Mathematics would no longer be a burdensome exercise in
mental discipline but would be sought as a practical way of
managing quantities.[78]

Instruction, under such conditions, could be carried forward
as a succession of direct experiences on the child's part. From
Rousseau, Dewey had learned that education was not some-
thing to be forced upon youth. It involved rather a process of
growth antedating the pupil's admission to the school and
extending beyond his departure from it. In teaching it was
essential always to take account of the conditions of learning,

to impart the ability to read, to write, and to use figures intelligently in terms that were themselves meaningful and real. That meant at the lower grades an emphasis on activities over abstractions, not as ends in themselves but as means of evoking stimulating questions.[79]

Learning would then become incidental to the process of dealing with authentic situations. Children who played at making things readily learned to weave, but in doing so began to wonder how cotton and wool came to be formed into their own garments. Those who had practice in electing a class president found it natural to inquire how the city elected a mayor.

The school was thus not simply to pander to a child's liking for interesting activities. It was to select those which led him on to a widening of significant achievements. Knowledge of geography, government, history, and arithmetic was acquired through the continual reconstruction of the student's own experiences. As he absorbed the significance of what he did, he was able to direct his attention to ever broader and more meaningful subjects. Furthermore, interest in the achievement of a practical end could steadily be transformed into interest in the process, that is into "thinking things out" intellectually or theoretically. The whole of education could thus be conceived as the process of learning to think through the solution of real problems.[80]

A school firmly oriented in the world of its pupils could dispense with discipline through the external force of keeping order. Children whose interest was actively engaged in their studies did not need policing. They could be permitted more than the usual amount of freedom, not for the purpose of relaxing real discipline, but to make possible the assumption of larger and less artificial responsibilities, the performance of which would evoke order from within.[81]

The establishment of voluntary patterns of obedience not only facilitated the teacher's task; it also emphasized that which was most important in education—its moral purpose. "All the aims and manners which are desirable in education are themselves moral. Discipline, natural development, culture, social efficiency, are moral traits—marks of a person who is a worthy member of that society which it is the business of education to further." Education was not simply a preparation for what would later be useful. It was more, "getting from the present the degree and kind of growth there is in it." From the very start therefore the child would become acquainted with, and through his life learn ever better, the relationship of knowledge to conduct. That was the most worthy function of his schooling.[82]

❦

THE RELEVANCE OF DEWEY'S CRITIQUE

Dewey's central conceptions of education are thus directly related to criticisms of the system that had developed in the United States between the time when he had ended his own schooling in Vermont and the time when he moved to Chicago. The conditions that evoked his revolt have changed radically since 1894; yet his comments have by no means lost their timeliness.

In some sixty years since the experimental school in Chicago opened its doors, John Dewey's ideas have had a profound effect upon American education. Despite the occasional errors in their application to practice and despite the distortions by uncritical enthusiasts, the schools have profited immensely from his influence.

There have been failings, but due largely through a disregard of the spirit of Dewey's intentions. In the hands of mediocre or incompetent teachers, new techniques have sometimes become ends in themselves. Dewey valued the experiment and the laboratory as means through which the pupil could learn by discovery. But when instruction is so routinized that the student knows from the manual what he will find before he puts his eye to the lens, the microscope has added nothing to his education. There is no point to substituting modern for ancient languages if dull teachers make one as dead as the other.

The danger of the abuse of techniques as ends in themselves has certainly been heightened by the tendency in many states to emphasize method over content in the preparation of the teacher. Yet Dewey always insisted that method could not be divorced from content. The subject matter and the means of communicating it were inextricably bound together; and a successful performance depended on the mastery of both. It is ironic now to find Dewey often blamed in retrospect for the proliferation of empty courses in "education" and for the "certification racket" that makes completion of a formal quota of methods courses the prerequisite to teacher licensing. "Consider the training schools of teachers," he wrote in 1899. "These occupy at present a somewhat anomolous position for thus they are isolated from the higher subject matter of scholarship, since, upon the whole, their object has been to train persons *how* to teach, rather than *what* to teach."[83]

Much of Dewey's writing was addressed to the problems of the elementary school, which in his day were most pressing. But neither at that nor at any other level did he regard familiarity with techniques as an alternative to command of the substance of subject matter. The two were inseparable at any level, for each acquired meaning from its relationship to the other.

Insofar as they are focused upon these abuses the complaints of the critics of Deweyism have a measure of validity. But the accusation that progressive education has kept Johnny from learning how to read or how to use a slide rule is unfounded and dangerous. It tends also to obscure the genuine improvements that have emanated from his influence.

In 1928, in an article on Soviet education, John Dewey pointed to the significance of the Russian achievement—far earlier than his detractors of thirty years later. But he did not then take, nor would he now have taken, technological proficiency or advances in rocketry as a test of the excellence of an educational system. He was certainly not impressed in the 1930's by the accomplishments of the Nazis in the same fields. Nor would he have overlooked in any comparison the counter-balancing achievements of our own educational system in medicine, in the peaceful branches of science, and in the humanities.[84]

The crucial test, rather, was the extent to which education served as a vital instrument teaching the individual to behave in the world about him. In his own society, Dewey warned that "academic and scholastic, instead of being titles of honor are becoming terms of reproach." He took that as a measure of the isolation of the schools and the negligence of the culture; and he feared that without an immediate reform schools would become empty and ineffective and the culture would be weakened from within. That accounted for the urgency with which he wrote.[85]

Dewey did not intend that his criticisms should become the creed of a sect or party; and he was uncomfortable when the label "Progressive" was attached to his ideas. He directed his revolt not against tradition but against a rather recent development—the gap created by the inability of Americans to adjust their conceptions of education and culture to the terms of the changing world about them. Unwilling to limit the scope of either education or culture by the lines of an artificial definition, he insisted upon broadening both by re-establishing their relationship to life.[86]

Late in life, reflecting upon the developments of a half-century, he made this clear, when he defined the new education as hostility to "imposition from above," to "learning from texts and teacher," to "acquisition of isolated skills and techniques by drill" to "preparation for a more or less remote future" and to "static aims and materials." Against those aspects of the school of the late nineteenth century he had called for the "expression and cultivation of individuality," for "learning through experience," and for "acquaintance with an ever-changing world."[87]

That much can be ascribed to the reaction against the trends of the 1880's and 1890's. But Dewey had no intention of proceeding entirely upon a basis of rejection. "When external authority is rejected," he pointed out in another connection, "it does not follow that all authority should be rejected, but rather that there is need to search for a more effective source of authority." In his times, the disjunction between the school and society had enshrined external and arbitrary authority in American education. His revolt, which is comprehensible in terms of his times, aimed to end that disjunction and sweep away that authority as a step in the reconstruction of education on a sounder basis.

NOTES

1. See Oscar Handlin, "Rejoinder to Critics of John Dewey," *New York Times Magazine,* June 15, 1958, p. 13; Lawrence A. Cremin, "The Progressive Movement in American Education: A Perspective," *Harvard Educational Review,* XXVII (1957), pp. 251 ff.
2. W. W. Folwell, "Public Instruction in Minnesota," National Education Association, *Addresses and Proceedings, 1875* (Salem, Ohio, 1875), pp. 63 ff.
3. A. C. McLaughlin, "History of Higher Education in Michigan," United States Bureau of Education, *Circular of Information, No. 4* (1891), pp. 175 ff.
4. J. L. Pickard, "Our Schools and Their Responsibilities," *Education,* XI (1891), pp. 480-481, 484; J. O. Reed, "Moral Aspects of Teaching," *The Academy, A Journal of Secondary Education,* V (1890), p. 204; *Youth's Companion,* August 21, 1890, p. 44, January 15, 1891, p. 36; *The School Arts Book,* IX (1909), pp. 290 ff.; W. F. Phelps, *The Teacher's Hand-Book for the Institute and the Class Room* (New York [1874]), pp. 15, 23.
5. A. D. Mayo, "Methods of Moral Instruction," National Education Association, *Addresses and Proceedings, 1872* (New York, 1873), pp. 18-19; O. T. Bright, "School Gardens," National Education Association, *Journal of Proceedings, 1903,* p. 84; Richard Jones, "Aids to Good Citizenship," *Educational Review,* XI (1896), pp. 233-234.
6. R. G. White, "The Public-School Failure," *North American Review,* CXXXI (1880), p. 549. See also Joseph Anderson in *Journal of Social Science,* XXXV (1897), p. 75; J. L. Pickard, "Our Schools and Their Responsibilities," *loc. cit.,* pp. 482, 488; "Editorial," *Education,* XI (1890), pp. 53 ff.; A. D. Mayo, "Methods of Moral Instruction," *loc. cit.,* p. 19; W. F. Phelps,

"Inaugural Address," National Education Association, *Addresses and Proceedings, 1876* (New York, 1877), p. 16; H. T. Bailey, "Arts and Crafts in Public Schools," *The School Arts Book*, VI (1907), pp. 365 ff.; Lucy L. W. Wilson, *Handbook of Domestic Science and Household Arts for Elementary Schools. A Manual for Teachers* (New York, 1900), p. viii; *Report of the* [Massachusetts] *Commission Appointed to Investigate . . . Manual Training* (Boston, 1893), pp. 59 ff., 79; J. E. Armstrong, "The Growing Encroachment of Social Life upon Study," *National Conference on Secondary Education* (Evanston, 1904), pp. 191-193.

7. C. W. Eliot, "Wherein Public Education Has Failed," *Forum*, XIV (1892), pp. 411, 412. See also Noah Porter, *The American Colleges and the American Public* (New Haven, 1870), p. 182.
8. G. L. Raymond, "Comments," *Journal of Social Science*, XXXVIII (1900), p. 132.
9. See E. D. Grizzell, *Origin and Development of the High School in New England before 1865* (New York, 1923), pp. 41 ff.; R. F. Butts and L. A. Cremin, *History of Education in American Culture* (New York, 1953), pp. 262 ff.; G. W. A. Luckey, *Professional Training of Secondary Teachers* (New York, 1903), pp. 57 ff.; I. L. Kandel, *History of Secondary Education* (Boston, 1930), p. 444; G. N. Kefauver, V. H. Noll, and C. E. Drake, "The Secondary School Population," United States Office of Education, *Bulletin, 1932*, No. 17, Monograph No. 4, pp. 2, 3.
10. H. K. Edson, "Classical Study . . . in the West," National Education Association, *Addresses and Proceedings, 1871* (New York, 1872), p. 161; W. J. S. Bryan, "Function of the Free Public High School," p. 54, and Charles de Garmo, "Comments," pp. 60 ff., *National Conference on Secondary Education* (Evanston, 1904); "Statement of President I. P. Gulliver," National Education Association, *Addresses and Proceedings, 1871* (New York, 1872), p. 167; N. M. Butler, "The Function of the Secondary School," *The Academy, A Journal of Secondary Education*, V (1891), pp. 133 ff.; I. L. Kandel, *op. cit.*, pp. 464 ff.
11. W. J. S. Bryan, "Function of the Free Public High School," *loc. cit.*, p. 53.
12. W. W. Folwell, "Public Instruction in Minnesota," *loc cit.*, pp. 65, 70; C. P. Cary, "Remarks," *National Conference on Secondary Education* (Evanston, 1904), p. 59.

13. National Education Association, *Report of the Committee of Ten on Secondary School Studies* (New York, 1894), p. 51. See also W. W. Folwell, "Public Instruction in Minnesota," *loc. cit.*, p. 63; A. M. Comey, "The Growth of New England Colleges," *Educational Review*, I (1891), pp. 209 ff.

14. H. K. Edson, "Classical Study . . . in the West," *loc. cit.*, pp. 162-163.

15. These arguments are summarized from E. S. Carr, "The Industrial Education of Women," National Education Association, *Addresses and Proceedings, 1876* (New York, 1877), pp. 241-245. See also S. N. D. North, "Industrial Education," *Journal of Social Science*, XXXIV (1896), pp. 29 ff.; J. L. Pickard, "Our Schools and Their Responsibilities," *loc. cit.*, p. 487; *Report of the* [Massachusetts] *Commission Appointed to Investigate Manual Training* (Boston, 1893), p. 63; *Report of the* [Massachusetts] *Commission on Industrial Education* (Boston, 1907), pp. 13-16, 38-40; F. H. Kasson, "The Typewriter," *Education*, XV (1895), p. 617; I. L. Kandel, *op. cit.*, pp. 417, 418, 458 ff.; E. D. Grizzell, *op. cit.*, pp. 277-279.

16. J. O. Reed, "Moral Aspects of Teaching," *loc. cit.*, p. 207; J. F. Brown, *The American High School* (New York, 1909), p. 115; "Manual Training in Schools," *Youth's Companion*, August 20, 1891, p. 453; "Prevention of Criminal Idleness," *Proceedings of the International Congress of Education, 1893* (New York, 1894), pp. 372 ff.; E. Davenport, *Education for Efficiency* (Boston, 1909), pp. 16, 28; *Report of the* [Massachusetts] *Commission Appointed to Investigate Manual Training* (Boston, 1893), p. 60.

17. D. G. Porter, "Perversion of Funds in the Land Grant Colleges," *Journal of Social Science*, XXXV (1897), pp. 77 ff.; *Report of the* [Massachusetts] *Commission Appointed to Investigate Manual Training* (Boston, 1893), pp. 65 ff., 72; *Report of the* [Massachusetts] *Commission on Industrial Education* (Boston, 1907), p. 43; J. T. Prince, *Second Report upon a Course of Studies for Elementary Schools* (Boston, 1898), pp. 23-24; United States Commissioner of Education, *Report*, 1892-1893, II, pp. 1423 ff.; P. H. Hanus, *Educational Aims and Educational Values* (New York, 1899), pp. 129 ff.

18. See, for example, the series, "Just the Boy That's Wanted," *Youth's Companion*, February, 1889. See also National Education Association, *Addresses and Proceedings, 1876* (New York, 1877), pp. 265 ff.; *The Century*, XLVI (1893), p. 475.

19. John Swett, "The Examination of Teachers," National Education Association, *Addresses and Proceedings, 1872* (Peoria, 1873), pp. 74, 75.
20. W. T. Harris, "Report of Committee to Report a Course of Study for All Grades," (July 12, 1876), National Education Association, *Addresses and Proceedings, 1876* (New York, 1877), pp. 60-61; A. D. Mayo, "Methods of Moral Instruction," *loc. cit.*, p. 12; E. G. Townsend, "The Text-Book Question," *Education*, XI (1891), pp. 556-557; W. W. Folwell, "Public Instruction in Minnesota," *loc. cit.*, p. 60; W. F. Phelps, *The Teacher's Hand-Book for the Institute and the Class Room* (New York [1874]), pp. 17, 27.
21. National Education Association, *Addresses and Proceedings, 1871* (St. Louis, 1872), p. 8. See also R. G. White, "The Public-School Failure," *loc. cit.*, pp. 537, 544.
22. W. P. Lyon, *Teachers' and Parents' Manual of Education* (New York, 1848), p. 63; S. J. May, "Address," *Memorial of the Quarter-Centennial Celebration of the Establishment of Normal Schools* (Boston, 1866), pp. 25 ff.; M. A. Whedon, "The Duty of Young People," *Education*, XV (1895), p. 358; Merle Curti, *Social Ideas of American Educators* (New York, 1935), pp. 19, 56-58.
23. W. F. Phelps, "Inaugural Address," p. 16, and Edward Olney, "The Country-School Problem," pp. 32 ff., National Education Association, *Addresses and Proceedings, 1876* (New York, 1877); G. T. Balch, *Methods of Teaching Patriotism in the Public Schools* (New York, 1890), p. vi; J. R. Buchanan, *New Education* (Boston, 1882), p. 296; W. T. Harris, "On A National University," National Education Association, *Addresses and Proceedings, 1874* (Worcester, 1874), pp. 84 ff.; H. T. Mark, *Moral Education in American Schools* (n.p., n.d.), p. 9.
24. L. Garde, "Comments," *Proceedings of the International Congress of Education, 1893* (New York, 1894), pp. 660 ff.; A. B. Foster, "Basketball for Girls," *American Physical Education Review*, II (1897), pp. 152-153; M. L. Pratt, "Physical Culture," *Education*, XV (1894), p. 218; J. B. McMaster, "Address," National Herbart Society, *Fourth Yearbook, 1898*, pp. 29-30; Merle Curti, *op. cit.*, pp. 251, 254.
25. John Hancock, "Speech," National Education Association, *Addresses and Proceedings, 1871* (New York, 1872), p. 220; Dr. Leverson, "Comments," *ibid.*, 1872 (Peoria, 1873), p. 174; Florence Kelley, in *Journal of Social Science*, XXXIV (1896),

p. 51; Richard Jones, "Aids to Good Citizenship," *Educational Review*, XI (1896), p. 243; H. E. Monroe, "A Substitute for Compulsory Education," *Education*, XIV (1894), p. 352.

26. *Youth's Companion*, July 2, 1891, p. 376; March 31, 1892, p. 162; August 18, 1892, p. 412; September 8, 1892, pp. 446, 447; October 13, 1892, p. 509; November 17, 1892.

27. *Youth's Companion*, February 6, 1890; G. T. Balch, *op. cit.*, pp. xi, 77 ff.; C. R. Skinner, *Manual of Patriotism for Use in the Public Schools of the State of New York* (Albany, 1904), *passim; Youth's Companion*, January 23, 1890, February 18, 1892. See also Merle Curti, *Roots of American Loyalty* (New York, 1946), pp. 133, 190 ff.

28. "Patriotism in the Schools," *Youth's Companion*, September 18, 1890, p. 488.

29. R. W. G. Welling, "Teaching of Civics," National Education Association, *Journal of Proceedings, 1903* (Winona, 1903), p. 99; Gustave Straubenmueller, "The Work of the New York Schools," pp. 177-180, and Paul Abelson, "Education of the Immigrant," pp. 163 ff., *Journal of the American Social Science Association*, XLIV.

30. *Education*, XI (1890-1891), pp. 572-573; *Youth's Companion*, June 5, 1890.

31. Henry James, *The Question of Our Speech* (Boston, 1905), p. 41; New England Association of Teachers of English, *Leaflet*, No. 79 (1910); "Our Schools' Greatest Task," *Youth's Companion*, June 19, 1890, October 13, 1892, p. 509; Lys d'Aimée, "Menace of Present Educational Methods," *Gunton's Magazine*, XIX (1900), pp. 263 ff.; John Bascom, "The Bennett Law," pp. 48 ff., and J. J. Mapel, "Repeal of the Compulsory Education Laws," pp. 54 ff., *Educational Review*, I (1891).

32. F. J. Kingsbury, "A Sociological Retrospect," *Journal of Social Science*, XXXIV (1896), p. 12; G. T. Balch, *op. cit.*, pp. viii, xxi; *The Century*, XLVI (1893), pp. 151, 635, 789, 952.

33. Frederick Guthrie, "Science Teaching," *Popular Science Monthly*, XLII (1893), pp. 520 ff.

34. See H. R. Douglass, *The High School Curriculum* (New York, 1956), pp. 13 ff.

35. National Education Association, *Report of the Committee of Ten on Secondary School Studies* (New York, 1894); W. T. Harris, "Report of Committee to Report a Course of Study for All Grades" (July 12, 1876), National Education Association,

Addresses and Proceedings, 1876 (New York, 1877), pp. 60-61. See, for example, H. K. Edson, "Classical Study . . . in the West," *loc. cit.*, p. 160.

36. C. W. Eliot, "Wherein Public Education Has Failed," *loc. cit.*, pp. 417, 423, 427; C. W. Eliot, "The Cultivated Man," National Education Association, *Journal of Proceedings and Addresses, 1903* (Winona, 1903), pp. 46 ff.

37. Wesley Mills, "The Natural or Scientific Method in Education," *Popular Science Monthly*, XLII (1892), p. 23.

38. J. F. Brown, *op cit.*, p. 106.

39. M. S. and Earl Barnes, *Studies in American History* (Boston, 1893), p. iii; M. S. Barnes, *Studies in American History. Teachers' Manual* (Boston, 1893); L. M. Salmon, "The Teaching of History in Academies," *The Academy, A Journal of Secondary Education*, V (1890), pp. 284-286; J. T. Prince, *op. cit.*, p. 21.

40. Daniel Quinn, "The Duty of Higher Education," p. 23, and S. T. Dutton, "Relation of Education to Vocation," pp. 57-58, *Journal of Social Science*, XXXIV (1896); P. H. Hanus, *op. cit.*, pp. 133 ff.

41. Lucy L. W. Wilson, *op. cit.*, pp. 5, 207, 270-271; L. K. Morss, "The Home Beautiful," *The School Arts Book*, IX (1909), pp. 104 ff.

42. A. D. Mayo, "Methods of Moral Instruction," *loc. cit.*, pp. 14 ff.

43. Lucy L. W. Wilson, *op. cit.*, p. 24, refers the student to Edith Wharton and Ogden Codman, Jr., *The Decoration of the House* (New York, 1897), in which, significantly, all desirable style is European.

44. A. D. Mayo, "Methods of Moral Instruction," *loc. cit.*, p. 21; "The Study of Music in Public Schools," United States Bureau of Education, *Circulars of Information*, No. 1 (1886), pp. 21-25; Frank Damrosch, "Music as an Ethical Factor in Community Life," *Journal of Social Science*, XLI (1903), p. 139.

45. William MacDonald, "What Return the Public May Expect from Public School Music," *Papers Read at the Institute for Supervisors of Music under the Direction of the Massachusetts State Board of Education, December 8, 1905* (Boston, 1906), pp. 7-9; M. E. Parker, *The Correlation of Music with Other Branches in the School Curriculum* (Boston, 1896), pp. 3, 11-13; *The Messenger* (official organ of the Music Teachers' National Association), V (1904), p. 412.

46. Edson Kemp, "Hettie's Musical Education," *Youth's Companion*, October 15, 1891.
47. E. B. Birge, *History of Public School Music* (Boston, 1928), pp. 147, 163, 205 ff., 249; C. H. Farnsworth, *Education Through Music* (New York, 1909), pp. 203 ff.
48. New England Conservatory of Music, *Calendar, 1891-1892* (Boston, 1891).
49. G. L. Raymond, "Influence of Art upon Education," *Journal of Social Science*, XXXVI (1898), pp. 105 ff.
50. H. M. Stanley, "Our Education and the Progress of Art," *Education*, XI (1890), p. 84; L. W. Miller, "High School Methods," *The School Arts Book*, VI (1906), pp. 85 ff.; H. T. Bailey, "The Fine Arts as an Ethical Factor in Community Life," *Journal of Social Science*, XLI (1903), pp. 128 ff.
51. *Journal of Social Science*, XXXVII (1899), p. 50.
52. C. D. Warner, *That Fortune* (New York, 1899), p. 288.
53. A. R. Kimball, "Education by Newspaper," *Journal of Social Science*, XXXVII (1899), pp. 30 ff.; Henry James, *op. cit.*, pp. 11 ff.; "The Differentiation of the High School Course in English," New England Association of Teachers of English, *Leaflet*, No. 91 (1911), pp. 3-5; A. R. Kimball, "Education by Newspaper," *loc. cit.*, p. 28; "What It Is To Be Educated," *Chautauquan*, XXX (1899), p. 19; "Correct Speech," *Youth's Companion*, May 24, 1894, p. 240.
54. W. A. Baldwin, "Course of Study in Drawing and Art," *The School Arts Book*, V (1906), p. 761; Lucy L. W. Wilson, *op. cit.*, pp. 3, 19; Isable Sewall, "A Course in Aesthetic Culture," *The School Arts Book*, V (1906), p. 585.
55. *Popular Science Monthly*, XLII (1893), pp. 453, 504, 821.
56. See Ward McAllister, *Society as I Have Found It* (New York, 1890), pp. 157 ff.; New England Association of Teachers of English, *Leaflet*, No. 79 (1910); Julia Ward Howe, *Is Polite Society Polite?* (Boston, 1895), pp. 3, 13, 15.
57. Edith Wharton and Ogden Codman, Jr., *op. cit.*, p. 5.
58. G. L. Raymond, "Influence of Art upon Education," *loc. cit.*, p. 113.
59. See, *e.g.*, C. M. Sheldon, *Edward Blake: College Student* (Chicago, 1900), p. 267.
60. W. B. Stewart, "Success in Practice," p. 324, and L. W. Fox, "Introductory Address," p. 366, *Medical Bulletin* (Philadelphia) XVI (1894); *A Protest Against the Medical Bill* (Boston, 1885), p. 2.

61. On earlier medical practice, see H. E. Sigerist, *American Medicine* (New York, 1934), pp. 131-132. On the emergence of the modern medical school, see especially Donald Fleming, *William H. Welch* (Boston, 1954).

62. J. F. Russell, "Why Law Schools Are Crowded," *Journal of Social Science*, XXXVII (1899), p. 164.

63. A. M. Douglas, "Larry," *Youth's Companion*, February 9, 1893, p. 70.

64. "Rich To-Day, Poor To-Morrow," *Youth's Companion*, March 23, 1893, p. 148.

65. North, "Industrial Education," *loc. cit.*, p. 31.

66. J. L. Pickard, "Our Schools and Their Responsibilities," *loc. cit.*, pp. 483-486; W. J. S. Bryan, "Function of the Free Public High School," *loc. cit.*, p. 53; F. W. Kelsey, "Future of the High School," *Educational Review*, XI (1896), p. 163.

67. F. S. Root, "The Educational Features of the Drama," *Journal of Social Science*, XXXV (1897), pp. 99 ff.

68. J. C. Dana, "The Relation of Art to American Life," *The School Arts Book*, VI (1906), p. 10.

69. See C. W. Eliot, "The Unity of Educational Reform," United States Commissioner of Education, *Report, 1892-1893*, II, pp. 1465 ff.; H. L. Boltwood, "The Growing Tendency to Imitate the Characteristic Features of College Life," *National Conference on Secondary Education and Its Problems* (Evanston, 1904), pp. 198-199; W. W. Folwell, "Public Instruction in Minnesota," *loc. cit.*, p. 71; *Education*, XI (1890-1891), p. 571; E. P. Seaver, "The Public High School," *Educational Review*, XIX (1900), p. 157; C. M. Smart, "Public Schools for the Privileged Few," *Arena*, X (1894), pp. 462 ff.

70. "Editorial," *Education*, XI (1891), pp. 638-639. See also the comments of Jane Addams, "Foreign-Born Children in the Primary Grades," National Education Association, *Journal of Proceedings and Addresses, 1897* (Chicago, 1897), pp. 107-110.

71. A. D. Mayo, "Methods of Moral Instruction," *loc. cit.*, pp. 12, 14; National Education Association, *Addresses and Proceedings, 1871* (St. Louis, 1872), pp. 9-10.

72. Sidney Hook, *John Dewey, an Intellectual Portrait* (New York, 1939), p. 13; Jerome Nathanson, *John Dewey* (New York, 1951), pp. 10 ff.; Max Eastman, *Heroes I Have Known* (New York, 1942), pp. 278 ff.

73. Willinda Savage, "John Dewey and 'Thought News,'" Claude Eggertsen, ed., *Studies in the History of Higher Education in*

Michigan (Ann Arbor, 1950), pp. 12 ff.; A. S. Whitney, *History of the Professional Training of Teachers at the University of Michigan* (Ann Arbor, 1931), pp. 34, 35; Max Eastman, *op. cit.*, pp. 291, 292.

74. P. A. Schilpp, ed., *The Philosophy of John Dewey* (New York, 1951), p. 452; Katherine Mayhew, *The Dewey School* (New York, 1936).

75. See, in general, G. R. Geiger, *John Dewey in Perspective* (New York, 1958); Morton White, *Social Thought in America* (Boston, 1957), pp. 94 ff.; P. A. Schilpp, *op. cit.*, pp. 419 ff.

76. John Dewey, *The School and Society* (Chicago, 1899), pp. 18-22.

77. John Dewey, *op. cit.*, pp. 38, 82 ff.

78. John Dewey, *op. cit.*, p. 113.

79. E. C. Moore, "John Dewey's Contributions to Educational Theory," *John Dewey, the Man and His Philosophy* (Cambridge, 1930), p. 23.

80. G. R. Geiger, *op. cit.*, pp. 197-198; Sidney Hook, *op. cit.*, pp. 177 ff.

81. John Dewey, *op. cit.*, pp. 124, 125; John Dewey, *Democracy and Education* (New York, 1916), p. 138.

82. John Dewey, *Democracy and Education*, pp. 362, 417; John Dewey, *School and Society*, pp. 124, 125; John Dewey, *Reconstruction in Philosophy* (New York, 1920), pp. 183-185.

83. John Dewey, *School and Society*, p. 80.

84. John Dewey, "Impressions of Soviet Russia IV: What Are the Russian Schools Doing?; V: New Schools for a New Era," *New Republic*, LVII (1928), pp. 64-67, 91-94; P. A. Schilpp, *op. cit.*, p. 471.

85. John Dewey, *School and Society*, p. 36.

86. R. F. Butts and L. A. Cremin, *op. cit.*, pp. 343 ff., 384; L. A. Cremin, "Revolution in American Secondary Education," *Teachers College Record*, LVI (1955), pp. 301 ff.

87. John Dewey, *Experience and Education* (New York, 1938), p. 56.